King Arthur's Return

Libris

KING ARTHUR'S RETURN

Celtic Art by Courtney Davis

Legends of the Round Table and Holy Grail Retraced

With text by
Helena Paterson

BLANDFORD

Paperback edition 1996

First published in the UK 1995 by Blandford
A Cassell Imprint
Cassell plc, Wellington House
125 Strand, London
WC2R 0BB

Distributed in the United States by Sterling Publishing Co., Inc.
387 Park Avenue South, New York, NY 10016-8810

Distributed in Australia by Capricorn Link (Australia) Pty Ltd
2/13 Carrington Road, Castle Hill, NSW 2154

British Library Cataloguing-in-Publication Data
A catalogue record for this book is available
from the British Library

ISBN 0-7137-2430-7 (hardback)
0-7137-2428-5 (paperback)

Typeset by Litho Link Ltd, Henfaes Lane, Welshpool, Powys, UK
Printed and bound in Hong Kong by Dah Hua Printing Press Co. Ltd

Contents

CONTENTS

Dedicated to all seekers of the Grail

Acknowledgements

First, I have to thank Helena Paterson for her text in this book, and also Ian Forrester Roberts for initially firing my imagination to create these images.

To all of my friends who helped me through my illness while completing this book, especially Dimity, Beatrice and Lawrence Stroud, and Michael and Janet Law.

To all of you who buy my books and have given me so much encouragement over the years with your kind letters.

May all of your Lights Shine!

COURTNEY DAVIS
Abbotsbury

Excalibur

Introduction

T*HE SPIRAL PASSAGE OF TIME MOVES* silently through the galaxy. The ritual calendar year in Celtic cosmology was an integral part of galactic time which embodied the lovely face of the Celts' great Lunar Goddess, Ceridwen, who controlled the destinies of all sun-kings and solar heroes. Her controlling hand of fate divided the ritual year into thirteen lunar months and symbolized the power of all ancient Fate Goddesses, whose interventions reminded mankind that their time on earth was limited and aligned to the changing light of the sun. This aspect of fate relates to the moon during its waning cycle, which forms part of the triple dimension of changing lunar light – new moon, full moon and dark moon.

King *Arthur's Return* begins by retracing his past life through a series of cameo scenes from the Arthurian saga which have been evoked by the power of the dark green crystal belonging to his sword, Excalibur. These adventures have been vividly re-created by Courtney Davis with great insight into the nature of the Holy Grail quest and the dark intrigues surrounding Arthur's court at Camelot. The accompanying text has been largely drawn from Thomas Malory's *Le Morte d'Arthur*, an acknowledged source of Arthurian material, which remains to date the most outstanding and fascinating account.

But, in order to relate to the new age of self-discovery, the text provides a more in-depth analysis of the spiritual nature of the Celts, which is as relevant today as it was in ancient times. The Arthurian legends are epic voyages of self-discovery which graphically record mankind's struggle to evolve on the spiritual level. The advent of Christianity among the Celts marked a spiritual watershed in their lives. It was a time when their ancient druidic religion was being confronted with a new sacrificial sun-king from the East, Jesus of Nazareth.

The Face of the Goddess, Gaia

Irish druids had long prophesied that the 'Son of Light' would one day appear in the British Isles in the West, and their Cornish cousins, another Celtic people, have always claimed that Joseph of Arimathea brought Jesus, as a young boy, to the druidic college at Place on the Roseland peninsula in Cornwall. This claim is no mere myth, for an account of his arrival was later recorded in the pictographs found on the arched stone doorway of the Saxon and Norman church at Place. Similar pictographs have been found on the doorway to the ancient temple at Denderah in Lower Egypt; they are esoteric symbols which relate to the cabbala and later Masonic signs. The site of the church had previously been a Celtic monastery and prior to that a convent. Long before then it was believed to have been the site of a druidic college and, even earlier, a Phoenician fort.

This strange thread of Celtic belief, that Jesus had once set foot on British soil, was later incorporated by the mystic poet and painter William Blake in his 'Jerusalem', which was to be immortalized as a stirring hymn. Between 1799 and 1827 Blake belonged to a druidic organization known as the Ancient Order of Druids and was their 'Chosen Chief', according to the records of Ross Nichols, a more recent

Chief Druid of the order. The Holy Grail legends in Thomas Malory's account were founded in the belief that Joseph of Arimathea had brought the cup or chalice used at the Last Supper, and later filled with Christ's blood, to the holy site at Glastonbury. In the Arthurian saga, Glastonbury, which had once been surrounded by the tidal waters of the sea, is referred to as the 'Isle of Avalon', where Arthur returned after he had been mortally wounded by Mordred.

Avalon retains a mystical aura in Arthurian legends which relates to earlier Celtic myths of the Otherworld realm – a kind of Celtic heaven where the old gods reside. As Arthur completes his journey of 'self-discovery', he then travels to the Celtic Otherworld and descends into the inner realm of Annwn, situated in the Underworld. This kingdom is ruled by Pwyll or Dis, an ancient Celtic God of the Underworld, a primal place where all earth life was formed and re-formed in the fiery abyss of Annwn. It was not, however, regarded as a place of eternal torment, as in the Christian concept of hell or purgatory. Although some souls had become entrapped there, according to Celtic belief, sun-kings such as Arthur could journey into Annwn and rescue them. This ancient belief predates the Christian teaching of a saviour who offered eternal life to his followers, and indeed all mankind.

It is not surprising, therefore, that modern druidic orders believe that the early mystical element of Christianity represented a fulfilment of druidic prophecy and belief. The last two chapters of the book bring the Arthurian saga full circle, back to the source of ancient Celtic beliefs which had laid the foundation for their conversion to Christianity. When

Arthur is reunited with Guinevere, the Arthurian saga is finally completed; but the unbroken thread of Celtic spiritual belief continues to weave its own magical tapestry in the hearts and minds of all races.

The Return of Arthur

THE SPIRIT OF KING ARTHUR, A CELTIC sun-king, remains imprisoned in a web of ancestral memory which still evokes a powerful sense of personal destiny. As the light of the solar year begins to return to earth after the winter solstice, the awakened spirit of King Arthur gazes into a crystal pool, the mirror of reflection that contains a record of all mankind's past deeds and glimpses of the future. The ephemeral presence of the great Celtic Goddess, Ceridwen, whose lovely face is serenely composed in meditation, draws him onwards across the chasm of time. In her hands she holds the spirit of King Arthur, as if frozen in time by a spell of enchantment. There is a new age of self-discovery stirring and there are new battles to be fought, but will she release him?

Roused from his deep slumber, Arthur boards a solar-ship steered by his loyal knight Bedivere and crosses the rainbow river which divides the earthly realm from the Celtic Otherworld, a place inhabited by the Sidhe, or Faery people, who represented the radiant and unearthly beauty of ancient gods. In Arthurian mysticism a Christianized concept of spiritual belief, Bedivere, was the 'Guardian of Mysteries', the recorder and witness. His role in druidism had originally been held by Swyedydd, the Chief Druid of Boudicca or Boadicea. This great Celtic Queen of the Iceni tribe nearly succeeded in driving the Romans out of Britain, but fate decreed otherwise.

The Mother

After her defeat, believed to be near Parliament Hill, London, the Romans pursued her – their leader, Suetonius Paulinus, boasting that he would send her to Rome in chains – but she mysteriously disappeared. As faithful Bedivere ministered to the mortally wounded King Arthur at Camelford Bridge in Cornwall, so Swyedydd at Battle Bridge near London attended his Queen. It is perhaps a significant fact that 'death' always took place near a river, which in Celtic myth – as in Greek myth with the River Styx – was a portal which flowed into the Underworld, the realm of the dead.

Legend has it that Boudicca committed suicide by taking a poison cup prepared by Swyedydd and her body was burnt, thus denying the enemy the satisfaction of displaying it or violating it by mutilation – a Roman custom. Her ashes were reputedly scattered on the tumulus on Parliament Hill that contained the bodies of her warriors. Thus her released spirit remained earthbound, as a haunting memorial empowered to inspire future defenders of Albion.

The Green Crystal

Arthur's solar-ship approaches the portal of time, and the mists of past ages, like waves, engulf his ship as he passes through the galactic vortex back to earth. He navigates with the aid of a magnetic silver fish, which contains a dark green crystal. Holding the dark crystal over the fiery abyss of Annwn, he gazes into the centre core of the earth's regenerative power, its volcanic heart. The dark green crystal belongs to his sword, Excalibur, which he must once again recover from the Lady of the Lake. The crystal represents the 'life-force' of the Celtic race, a potent energy symbolically regenerated every solar year.

As the boat emerges on the other side of the time portal, Arthur has resumed his dual role and earthly disguise as the 'Lame Fisher King', whose maiming had laid the kingdom to waste until the Grail was won. Arthur's malaise was caused by Guinevere's love for Lancelot, whose very name signifies a wounding spear or lance. Lameness has a sacred connection with all ancient Smith Gods, such as Vulcan, a Roman deity, and Govannon the Celtic God of the Forge. Lameness represented the mortality aspect or human impediment, and the alchemy of smithcraft or transmuting metals, also symbolized in the transformation of the human soul into a divine spark of creation.

The Grail King

In druidism, the ancient religion of the Celts, the 'Circle of Creation', known as Gwynved, had three separate stages of evolution. The earthly stage was referred to as the 'Circle of Abred', which symbolized 'Trial', when the evolving soul was still earthbound. Arthur's sword, Excalibur, was a symbol of both their superior knowledge of metal-working and their spiritual belief in the immortality of the human soul – a victory over earthly death. Excalibur was a gift from the great Mother Goddess, Ceridwen, who appeared as the Lady of the Lake in Arthurian myth. Arthur must therefore recover his sword and, by doing so, re-enact the primeval saga of life and death in order that mankind can continue to evolve.

The Lady of the Lake

As ARTHUR GAZES INTO THE DARK crystal, a mirror reflection of the Lady of the Lake appears at his side, holding aloft the sword Excalibur. He holds the 'Scales of Justice', which symbolize his divine right to administer Justice on earth – wielded by the power of the sword in just hands. The laws of knightly chivalry and justice for all epitomized the Order of the Round Table. When the first Celts arrived in Ireland, they brought with them four treasures which symbolized their superiority over all other races. The Invincible Sword of Lugh, a solar deity, was one of these treasures, and it became the prototype of all other magical swords in Celtic myth. The Sword of Lugh, which sang, later belonged to Ireland's greatest warrior, Cuchulain, then reappears as Excalibur in Welsh and Breton myth.

The sword represents an ancestral memory of a warrior race that had learned science and craftsmanship from mysterious sages enthroned in the great cities of Falias, Gorias, Fineas and Murias – said to lie beneath the sea. This link with an Atlantean civilization permeates Celtic myths and perhaps explains the association with supernatural beings who continued to dwell in lakes and rivers. In Irish Celtic myth, wisdom was obtained by eating the king of all river fish, the salmon. The radiant divinity of their ancient gods was identified with the four children of Lir, a Sea God, who were transformed into four white swans. These graceful water birds have long been associated with the British monarchy, which made laws to protect them, and to this day certain swans remain the 'property of the reigning monarch'.

The dark crystal recalls the lakeside scene of Arthur receiving the ancient symbol of power with Merlin at his side. But the power of the sword has evolved, along with Celtic belief, and Merlin instructs Arthur to guard its scabbard well, for it represents his mortal life and the wisdom to wield the sword justly. Arthur had foolishly remarked that he preferred the power of the sword, a sign of human frailty which symbolized the weakness or Achilles' heel of all sun-kings.

The Sword

When the scabbard was stolen by Morgan le Fay, Arthur's kingdom began to crumble into civil war and famine. Although he finally defeats his enemies, he succumbs to a mortal blow from his treacherous nephew, Mordred, who is really his son. Merlin's warning had not been heeded, but Arthur's demise is part of the saga of the sacrificial nature of a Celtic sun-king.

Twilight is the time when supernatural forces begin to weave their magic, for it marks the decreasing solar light in the sky. As Arthur stands in the boat on the shimmering lake, the sun slowly sinks beneath the horizon and the waters of the lake reflect a golden hue. The Fisher King's net has been cast upon the lake in an attempt to capture the elusive prize of wisdom – a symbolic reminder that Arthur must regain his kingdom and master his human weakness. The Arthurian saga primarily represents mankind's quest for immortality, and Arthur must, therefore, confront his past in order to win back Guinevere, who represents the fleeting time of twilight in the ritual year.

The Lady in the Lake

The Face of Merlin

When Arthur drew the sword from the stone, another of the four treasures that identified the true king, he assumed his rightful place as ruler of ancient Britain. Merlin, his chief druid and master magician, was a shadowy figure who secretly advised and instructed Arthur in the arts of kingship. It was Merlin who devised the test to determine the rightful king and it was through his magical skills that Arthur was conceived. Merlin's role relates to the power of the druids, which remained in place long after the Celts were Christianized. Arthur's meeting with the Lady of the Lake represents a continuing thread of Celtic spiritual belief in the supernatural power of the ancient Lunar Goddess.

Merlin, great magician though he was, became imprisoned in a cave under a huge rock through the enchantment of Vivien, whom he had unwisely attempted to rape. Vivien, 'a damosel of the lake' in Arthurian myth, cleverly thwarts his advances and tricks him into telling her many of his arcane secrets. But she is, of course, none other than the Lunar Goddess, for only the Goddess could outwit Merlin. This age-old adversity is an ancestral memory recalling the power struggle between the Celt's matriarchal culture and invading patriarchal tribes. The romantic title

'The Lady of the Lake' was created by Thomas Malory, who resurrected the Arthurian myths during the Wars of the Roses, when the bardic tradition was beginning to flourish once again and it seemed there would be a Welsh dynasty on the English throne.

Arthur and Guinevere

THE IMAGERY EVOKED BY THE DARK crystal returns to earlier scenes and Arthur is suddenly overwhelmed at the sight of his first meeting with Guinevere. Her father, King Leodegrance of Cameliard, had been besieged by King Rience of North Wales, an old enemy of Arthur, who was always conspiring against him. Leodegrance, on the other hand, had been a staunch supporter and a loyal friend to Arthur's father, Uther Pendragon. On hearing news of the siege, Arthur immediately summoned King Ban and King Bors, and together they departed with a great army to rescue Leodegrance. The three kings soundly defeated Rience and the people of Cameliard hailed them as great and noble knights. As

Arthur rode triumphantly into Leodegrance's castle, he first set eyes on Guinevere, who shyly greeted him. Arthur had never seen such a fair young maiden, and ever after he loved her.

It was a brief encounter, but Arthur was determined that one day he would wed Guinevere and make her his queen. Several years were to pass, because of his duties as king, before he could fulfil this secret pledge, but when his barons requested that he should take a wife, Arthur told Merlin of his choice. Merlin, however, warned Arthur that, though Guinevere was indeed the fairest lady in the land, she would love another and this would cause him great sorrow and provoke dissent among his knights. But Arthur was becoming weary of the burdens placed upon him as king, and longed for Guinevere with great passion. And so, after obtaining Leodegrance's blessing, Guinevere was delivered to Merlin with her wedding gift of the Round Table and a hundred loyal knights from Cameliard.

Arthur and Guinevere

The Round Table had been given to Leodegrance by Uther Pendragon for safekeeping, and thus it was restored to King Arthur's court and Merlin found fifty more knights to make up the Order of the Round Table. Merlin then began to prophesy the adventures of the Sangreal, their quest for the Holy Grail. This Arthurian legend is perhaps the most famous in the world, for it incorporates the aspirations of all religions – the search for eternal life or immortality, which can be accomplished only when the evolved soul reaches divine union with the creator or creatrix. The legend of the Holy Grail quest was, however, drawn from the ancient well of Celtic belief.

The third of the four treasures belonging to the Celts when they invaded Ireland was the Cauldron of Dagda, which is referred to as the Cauldron of Ceridwen in Welsh bardism. The cauldron symbolized spiritual fulfilment or initiation and could restore dead warriors back to life. Its rim was set with nineteen pearls, and it was reputedly made from rare and precious metals and was warmed by the breath of nine virgins. Nine is the sacred number of the great Lunar Goddess, Ceridwen, and nineteen is the number of years which make up a great lunar year, a sacred division of

The Wedding

universal time and the foundation of the Celtic ritual calendar year. The real prize or magical content of the cauldron was believed to be 'Prophecy', which relates to ancient druidic initiation ceremonies, when cauldrons brewed sacred potions.

The Round Table was said by Merlin to represent both the solar year or zodiac and the world. King Arthur and Queen Guinevere in druidic cosmology represented the dual principle of polarities – the pivotal principle of light and darkness which provided the alternating impetus in all creation. Arthur was identified with the vernal equinox and Guinevere with the autumnal equinox. Thus Merlin's warning had a more profound meaning or implication. Arthur, like all sun-kings, could claim his bride only fleetingly during the two days of the equinoxes when day and night were equally balanced. Arthur and Guinevere in esoteric terms represent the dual soul of mankind, which in druidic cosmology was identified with the rising and setting sun.

The Face of Guinevere

Merlin therefore knew that any bride Arthur chose would be someone who was destined to leave him, as day cannot live with night. The dissent of his knights symbolized a threatened discord of 'Time' in the ritual calendar year that would have come to pass if Arthur and Guinevere had achieved permanent union together. Although there is some historical evidence of a sixth-century Arthur or Arturus, a Romanized Celt who defeated the Saxon and Viking invaders of Celtic Britain after the departure of the Roman legions, the astronomical principle associated with Arthur is a prime druidic cosmic myth with a more ancient origin.

The beautiful face of Guinevere, which haunted Arthur as a young man, symbolizes the lovely face of the Goddess – the matriarchal creatrix who maintained the harmony of the universe and the seasons on earth in her triple role as maiden, mother and matron. In Arthurian legend, the body of Arthur was borne away on a barge with three weeping queens in attendance; they were veiled, which alludes to this ancient trinity.

Morgan le Fay

THE DARK CRYSTAL BEGINS TO VIBRATE with a magnetic force and Arthur senses a disturbing but familiar presence. The imagery changes as the form of Morgan le Fay casts her dark shadow. His half-sister in her role as Fate Goddess represents the darker aspects of the human soul which need to be confronted and therefore must be acknowledged. The Celtic Fate Goddess took many forms. As the Irish Morrigan, she assumed the terrifying shapes of sea-serpents and monstrous beings. As Morgan le Fay, in Arthurian myth, she conspired against Arthur secretly and with great subtlety. It was Morgan who stole the sacred scabbard of Excalibur, thus rendering Arthur vulnerable; this is the role of all Fate Goddesses.

Morgan le Fay

In Arthurian myth the reason for her concealed hatred of Arthur was a desire to exact a timely vengeance for the death of her father, the Duke of Cornwall, who had been cruelly dispatched by King Uther Pendragon. For Uther had desired the Duke's lovely wife, Igraine, and thus made war on him in order to satisfy his lust. Morgan had been sent to a nunnery, and there she learned from forbidden books the arts of necromancy and other arcane lore. She later married King Uriens of Gore, who became a loyal friend to Arthur. Their friendship angered Morgan and she tried unsuccessfully to murder her husband on many occasions. Arthurian myths are full of intriguing sagas which are often difficult to untangle, but they provide a wealth of creative inspiration.

Mordred was believed to be the foster son of Morgan le Fay, but he was really Arthur's son by his half-sister Queen Margawse of Orkney – an incestuous relationship in which Arthur, who was unaware at the time that Margawse was his sister, unwittingly fathered a child who would one day rise against him. Too late, Merlin warned Arthur of this threat and advised him to put to death all the male babies born on May Day. So Arthur cast the infants adrift in a boat, knowing they would perish at sea. A foul deed for a Christian knight and

Arthur and Mordred

king even to consider, apart from its strange connection with the deeds of the biblical Herod, it also conforms to a more ancient Celtic myth in which the Bardic God Taliesin, a solar deity, was cast adrift by his mother, the great Lunar Goddess, Ceridwen. Taliesin had tricked the Goddess into conceiving him, but survived, as befits all solar deities.

May Day was the Celtic fire festival of Beltane, which in darker times was, it is believed, celebrated with human sacrifices by the druids. Mordred had also survived his ordeal and thus began an unholy alliance with Morgan to violently overthrow Arthur and seize the throne – he was, after all, the King's son, conceived through sinful means, just like his father before him. Mordred, unlike Taliesin, was not a radiant sun-king, but has assumed the persona of Avagddu, Ceridwen's first-born son, who was the Dark Twin of the solar deity.

In one very ancient Celtic myth, Avagddu appears as Hafgan, the co-ruler with King Arawn of the Underworld. They are bitter enemies and King Arawn persuades Pwyll, Lord of Dyfed, to change places with him in order to defeat Hafgan. Pwyll duly completes this task and kills Hafgan, and thus becomes the Dark Initiator into the mysteries of Annwn. In parallel world myths, Pwyll is a Celtic Pluto or Set, the treacherous brother of the Egyptian King Osiris – another sacrificial solar deity and tree spirit whom Arthur resembles. Pwyll or Dis in Celtic myth is, however, regarded as the 'Guardian' of Annwn, the primal fire and source of immortality.

In the last battle between Arthur and Mordred, said by some Arthurian scholars to have taken place on Salisbury Down, Arthur offered Mordred a truce and lands in his kingdom. He was loath to kill Mordred, having painfully discovered that he was his son. How could he blame Mordred for rising against him when he had sought to murder him as an infant? Indeed, the Fate Goddess Morgan le Fay had carried out her devious plans only to set in motion the laws of retribution which, though evoking a more severe form of justice, was often a necessary penalty.

Fate was not to be denied. Though Mordred had consented to a truce, as the two armies faced each other in an uneasy stand-off, a viper bit one of Mordred's men standing close to Arthur. The knight drew his sword to kill the serpent, but Arthur's knights, believing there was treachery afoot, immediately drew their swords and a bloody battle commenced. The tragic consequences resulted in both Mordred and Arthur receiving mortal blows from each other. Thus a Celtic kingdom was destroyed by a potent symbol of fate, but the spear thrust into Mordred by Arthur relates to the last of the four treasures of the Celts – the magical Spear of Finias. The following chapter reveals the powerful symbolism associated with this spear.

The Double Head of Merlin

But where was Merlin? There is no mention of him in the twilight reign of Arthur. He remains the true mystery figure in Arthurian myth, as a link with the Celt's druidic religion and the mystical nature of Celtia or the Otherworld realm. Druidism, like Merlin, had to go 'underground' in order to survive the persecution of Christian zealots. Thomas Malory, another mysterious figure in fifteenth-century England, was also in prison when he wrote the first account of the Arthurian myth in English, published by Caxton. It has remained a 'best-seller' ever since and is an acknowledged account, albeit from an unknown source.

Arthur Perceives His Destiny

AN EERIE SILENCE SURROUNDS ARTHUR as the light emanating from the dark crystal briefly dims like a flickering candle. The sky darkens and the earth below him shakes violently, and the abyss of Annwn roars with a fiery breath. Arthur feels a searing pain pierce his side and he is unable to move. Summoning all his courage and faith, he makes the sign of the cross. A prism of light suddenly appears on the distant horizon. The scene of Christ's Crucifixion spreads across the world as though projected on a gigantic screen. But he can hardly bare to look at the agony of the cosmic Christ, who represents the suffering of the world in all religions – the torment of the universal soul.

The Lance

The two women weeping at the foot of the Cross, Christ's mother Mary and the Magdalene, symbolize the grief of the Goddess. The Roman centurion, still holding the spear that had pierced Christ's side, stands bowed, ashamed to look at what has been done that day. His name was Gaius Cassius (later known as Longinus) and he was the captain of the Temple Guard. He carried the spear of Herod as the symbol of his authority, which, according to Judaic records, had been forged under the direction of Phineas, an ancient prophet. It symbolized the magical powers inherent in the blood of God's chosen people, and as a talisman of power it had been raised in the hand of Joshua when he signalled his soldiers to shout down the walls of Jericho. It was also, reputedly, the same spear hurled at young David by King Saul in a fit of jealousy.

The Crucifixion scene begins to fade away into the shape of a huge golden eagle, as the dark crystal projects another brilliant stained-glass-window reflection of the past. Arthur is back at Camelot, and sitting at a desk is one of his scribes busily at work as the King attends to matters of state. This day had been like any other day, but something had occurred which remained deeply locked in Arthur's memory.

He had been making plans for his wedding with Guinevere, and quietly brooding on Merlin's warning. There was a sudden flapping noise at the window and a golden eagle appeared, hovering outside. The scribe seemed not to notice it, but as Arthur stared at this bird of omen he felt a great inner sense of pending doom.

*G*olden eagles in Celtic myth were believed to hold the souls of sun-kings and later became identified with the souls of Christian saints. Realizing the significance of this omen, a sign of his own mortality, Arthur was greatly alarmed that it should occur at such a time. He had never doubted Merlin's wisdom or power of prophecy, but Merlin had also foretold the wondrous adventures of the Knights of the Round Table and their quest for the Holy Grail. And this Order could be established only when the Round Table was restored to Arthur by Guinevere as her wedding gift.

The Bird of Omen

He ponders the dilemma but briefly, for the imagery moved swiftly onwards. Arthur stands holding the spear of Longinus, the body of Christ lies at his feet. This miraculous vision evoked by the spirit of the golden eagle has given Arthur the faith and courage to pursue his destiny. His role as sacrificial sun-king has been defined as fulfilling his true role on earth – that of 'The Spearman'. He now knows that when he thrust the spear into Mordred's body, he saved his kingdom from the forces of evil. Though his kingdom was destroyed, from its ashes rose a Christian nation; for had Mordred ruled, ancient Britain would have stayed for ever in the Dark Ages.

The spear of Herod played a decisive role in the mystical element of the Crucifixion, for when the Temple Guard arrived on the scene, it was to permit the Jewish high priests to crush the bones of Jesus of Nazareth while he still lived. The high priests were determined to avert the prophecy of Isaiah relating to their Messiah: 'A bone of Him shall not be broken.' Gaius, deeply impressed with the manner and humility of Jesus, decided to protect his body by thrusting the spear into his right side. Thus, by killing him, the cruel mission of the priests was thwarted.

Arthur and the Spear of Destiny

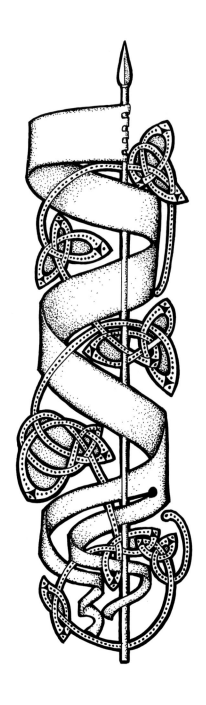

Gaius became a Christian convert and revered as a saint in the first Christian community in Jerusalem, and he was known as Longinus, 'The Spearman'. For not only was he a prime witness to the shedding of Christ's blood of the New Covenant, but his action triggered a catalyst of revelation which enabled the Resurrection. As legend around the spear grew, it became a symbol of the New Covenant and future Christian kings such as Charlemagne were believed to have possessed it; for whoever held it, held the destiny of the world in his hands for good or evil.

The Quest for the Holy Grail

ARTHUR'S ATTENTION IS MOMENTARILY distracted from gazing into the dark crystal by the sound of approaching horsemen and the shrill blast of heralds' trumpets. The noise reaches a deafening climax, then disperses into a distant echo. The imagery of the crystal reveals two knights of the Round Table galloping through the Perilous Forest in search of the Holy Grail. Arthur recognizes Sir Galahad and Sir Percival, who would later be joined by Sir Bors and succeed in their quest. They had followed Sir Lancelot, who found the chapel where the Grail was lodged, but at first he could see no entrance and camped outside. During the

Childe Percival

night he had a vision of the Grail, but was warned not to enter the chapel. Though Lancelot was the best warrior and the most courteous knight in Christendom, his love for Guinevere was regarded as a mortal sin, a flaw which denied him the Grail.

Galahad, his son by the Lady Elaine, was regarded as the 'Perfect Knight', the best knight in the world, a distinction which placed him above the earthly dimension of spirit. Sir Percival de Galis, the son of King Pellinore of the Isles, became one of the greatest knights of the Round Table and a Grail winner. The story of Percival's lineage and of his heroic adventures bear a striking resemblance to that of the Greek hero Perseus – a common phenomenon when comparing Greek and Celtic myths. Percival's son, Lohengrin, became associated with the swan legends, an ancient source of Celtic myth, which referred to the Celt's mysterious origins. Sir Bors de Ganis, regarded as the 'Noblest Knight', was a kinsman of Sir Lancelot. It was Sir Bors who defended Queen Guinevere when she was accused of treason by Sir Mador.

Galahad

The wondrous imagery of the Grail legend assumes a colourful tapestry, with the deeds of Galahad taking centre-stage. Galahad was descended, through his mother, from a truly mystical line associated with Joseph of Arimathea. As well as slaying wicked knights and demons, his heroic deeds also included healing the sick and restoring the dead to life – a miraculous power not given to other great knights. When Galahad arrived at Camelot to become a knight of the Round Table, there was already great excitement at court due to the strange news of a sword found sticking in a great rock in a nearby river. All the knights assembled there and marvelled at the sight of a red marble stone with a richly jewelled sword inscribed in letters of gold. It read: 'Never shall man take me hence, but only he by whose side I ought to hang, and he shall be the best knight of the world.'

When King Arthur saw the letters he immediately declared that the sword belonged to Lancelot, who wisely, but graciously, declined. The King then commanded his nephew, Sir Gawain, to withdraw the sword, but to no avail. Percival was likewise commanded, but he knew the sword did not belong to him, and thus it remained. They were interrupted by the arrival of an old hermit dressed in white; although none

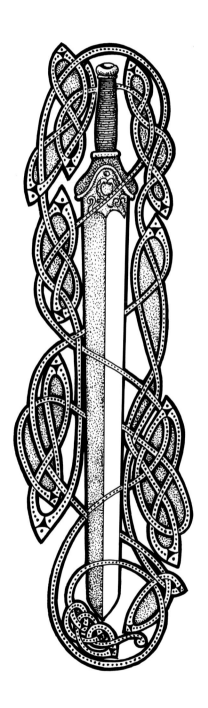

knew him, he was, of course, Merlin in disguise. With him came a young knight, in red arms and without a sword or shield, save an empty scabbard hanging by his side. Having acquainted the assembly with the young knight's lineage, the hermit then declared that this same day would mark the start of the adventures of the Holy Grail.

King Arthur therefore requested that Galahad should try to draw the sword. This he did, and it appeared to fly out of the stone at his light touch. Thus Galahad was armed, but he was still without a horse and shield. How Galahad obtained the shield of Joseph of Arimathea is part of Grail legend, but when he rode out from Camelot on this holy quest, Queen Guinevere presented him with a fine steed. She had been grieved to learn of his birth, for Lancelot had sworn to love no other maiden. But on meeting Galahad, whose features and manner so resembled his father's, she had immediately loved him.

The Question

Galahad, on the fourth day after leaving Camelot, came upon the White Chapel and met up with other knights of the Round Table, who told him that within the chapel lay a shield which no man could bear lest it kill or maim him. The shield was pure white with a red cross made from the blood of Joseph, the son of Joseph of Arimathea, who had prophesied that none other than Galahad, the last of his line, shall bear it. Galahad was therefore a Holy Knight of the Cross. When Galahad eventually found the Grail, the holy chalice and the spear of Longinus lay upon a silver table, and he was annointed with the blood of the spear and fed from the holy chalice.

With Sir Percival and Sir Bors, he departed in a strange ship and sailed to the realm of the Fisher King, where Galahad healed the maimed king with the holy vessels. With the quest of the Sangreal completed, he asked God to release his earthbound spirit. His soul thus departed the earthly kingdom, and as it ascended, so the Holy Grail and spear vanished before the eyes of Percival and Bors.

The Cauldron

Guinevere and Lancelot

WHILE ARTHUR REMAINS LOCKED INTO the wondrous vision of the Grail, the dark crystal is already beginning to reflect a less dazzling light. A more sombre scene appears, revealing Arthur seated at the Round Table with faithful Bedivere by his side. Guinevere, her face turned away from Arthur, stands weeping as a grave-faced Lancelot departs from court. For the sake of keeping the peace among Arthur's knights, Lancelot had decided to return to his own lands across the sea – the land of the Joyous Gard. A division of loyalties had started to fester because of the Queen's apparent love for Lancelot, which had come to a head when Guinevere had been falsely accused of trying to poison Sir Gawain. Lancelot had been absent from court and unable to defend her, and thus his kinsman Sir Bors became her champion.

News had reached Lancelot, who hastily returned to court in disguise and took Sir Bors's place to challenge Sir Mador, the Queen's accuser, whom he defeated in single combat and thus, according to the law of trial, acquitted the Queen of blame. But once again, with a heavy heart, he decided to leave court as he loved the King and was determined not to be the cause of such dissent. Sir Gawain, Arthur's nephew, was a vengeful knight and Lancelot knew that if he stayed, one day he would have to confront Gawain and he was loath to slay a knight of the King's blood. Lancelot was the son of King Ban of Benwick, but as a child he had been adopted by a queen who resided in a watery realm under a great lake, hence his name, Lancelot du Lac. Arthur remained gazing at the figures of Lancelot and Guinevere as they both disappear into shadows.

The Round Table

The imagery evoked by the dark crystal returns to past scenes of Camelot, and Arthur is confronted with the painful memory of Guinevere being embraced by Lancelot. In splendid isolation, he sits upon his throne, as the flames of jealousy and passion separate him from the two people he loved best in all his kingdom. He had been cruelly tricked this time by his half-sister, Morgan le Fay, into believing that Guinevere had been an unfaithful wife. Her love for Lancelot and his devotion to her had been skilfully manipulated by Morgan in order to cause dissent and disorder among his knights, thus rendering his kingdom weak and divided – a clever scheme which enabled Mordred to mount a violent campaign against Arthur in an attempt to seize the throne.

The plight of Arthur is an ongoing saga in Celtic myth, resembling that of King Eochy of Ireland and his bride Etain. King Eochy had married a young maiden who really belonged to the Otherworld realm, and she was already the wife of King Midir, who eventually reclaimed her. Lancelot's foster mother, the Queen of the Lake, had endowed him with supernatural powers which made him a great knight, but he could not win the Grail, for it also represented the dividing line of Christianity with earlier pre-Christian beliefs. Lancelot remains the 'Champion' of the Goddess, whose status was becoming increasingly diminished.

Guinevere and Lancelot

In ancient Celtic cosmology the ritual year was symbolized by the Triune Queen, Ceridwen, the creatrix who bears the sun-king at the winter solstice. In her triple role as mother, sister and lover, she controls the destiny of the sun-king. In Arthurian myth Lancelot was cast as the paramour or 'Lover' of Guinevere instead of Arthur, the sun-king. This 'change of roles' appears to signify a change of loyalties or beliefs but is, in fact, quite the reverse, for in ancient Celtic myths the Lunar Goddess reigned supreme and never shared her throne with a husband. King Arthur therefore represents the 'Challenger' of the Goddess, for the sun-king had become a Christian knight.

As Lancelot departs into the swirling waters of the Otherworld, Arthur begins to realize once again how easily he had been tricked by Morgan. Also, he had not heeded the advice of Merlin, who warned him not to marry Guinevere, and thrice he had failed to protect her: when she had been falsely accused of treason, at another time abducted by Sir Meliagrance, and then finally condemned to the stake for adultery. His actions symbolize the initial dilemma of the Celts, who faced the prospect of having to choose between their old gods and the new Christian God.

Lancelot Riding Forth

Although the Celts had numerous gods and goddesses, it must be remembered that at the centre of their religious doctrine was a unique belief in an invisible and indestructible creator or creatrix who had empowered mankind's soul with immortality – a belief which caused derision among the early Romans and even ancient Greeks. Only in pre-dynastic Egypt and ancient Judaea did such an unusual and outrageous belief exist. The Greeks and Romans, and all other ancient races in the Old World, believed that only the gods were immortal. Reincarnation, or the metempsychosis of souls, preached by the druids actually predated similar beliefs held by Pythagoras.

The Vengeance of Mordred and Agravaine

THE LIGHT OF THE DARK CRYSTAL AGAIN begins to dim as the changing scene reveals two knights standing on either side of a mighty oak, which has imprisoned the soul of Arthur, the sun-king. Agravaine and Mordred were half-brothers, their mother being Queen Margawse of Orkney, who was the sister of King Arthur. Agravaine was also a brother to Sir Gawain, who, though suspicious of the nature of the relationship between Lancelot and Guinevere, had great respect for Lancelot's prowess as a knight. Lancelot had saved his life and, on numerous occasions, the life of the King, whom Gawain loved dearly. But Agravaine was determined to expose

Guinevere as an unfaithful wife, despite Gawain's warning that such a scandal would rend the kingdom in two. He was also mindful that Guinevere was a great queen.

Arthur continues to gaze into the dark crystal, as he remembers only too well the action of these two cowardly knights who were of his blood. He could understand Mordred's vengeful nature, and had long been wary of his brother-in-law King Lot, Agravaine's father, who had opposed Arthur's claim to the throne. Agravaine had the same proud and unyielding nature as his father, but Gawain, though hot-headed, had learned to curb his impulsive actions and was a true and loyal knight to Arthur.

In Celtic myth, tree spirits were archetypal gods and oak-tree spirits were identified with sacrificial sun-kings. The treachery of Mordred and the hatred of Agravaine for Lancelot and Guinevere thus enabled a deadly conspiracy to be forged, effectively setting in motion the death of Arthur. But sun-kings

Two Vengeful Knights

such as Arthur can never be destroyed, for their spirit remains locked into the national psyche, or ancestral memory. The mighty oak has long been bound up with the history of the British Isles and has royal connections through heraldry and coinage.

The scene changes, as though an invisible hand is turning the pages of memory with increasing urgency, for the powers of the dark crystal are limited. The reflective imagery now reveals a scene of dark mischief and intrigue. Mordred and Agravaine have met up with each other in a dark forest, as the woeful full moon casts an ominous light. Mordred was eager to persuade Agravaine to approach the King with his suspicions of Guinevere's adultery. Thus they conspired, and it was agreed that Agravaine would inform the King and, in order to obtain proof, advise him to tell Guinevere that he would be away hunting on a certain night. Agravaine convinced the King, who was reluctant at first to enter into such subterfuge, but Agravaine had argued that if the Queen was innocent, then Arthur would have nothing to reproach himself with.

Mordred and Agravaine

Agravaine and Mordred had, however, under the direction of Morgan, wickedly devised to send a message to Lancelot informing him that the Queen wished to speak with him in her bedchamber. Sir Bors, Lancelot's kinsman, ever alert and wary of a plot, warned Lancelot not to attend the Queen at such a late hour with the King absent from court. But Lancelot, always brave and fearless, was determined to go to the Queen, whose life might have been in danger. Agravaine and Mordred remained secretly concealed close by, with twelve other knights, ready to trap him. Whilst Arthur had agreed to Agravaine's request for an escort, he had also ordered that Lancelot and the Queen must not be harmed.

Mordred and Agravaine, however, intended to kill both Lancelot and the Queen. Court etiquette forbade any knight to approach the Queen in her bedchamber armed. They knew, therefore, that Lancelot would be unarmed and, with this advantage, they planned to kill them both; they were well aware that Guinevere was still greatly loved by the King and, if left alive, would undoubtedly accuse them of murdering an unarmed Lancelot.

The Face of Lancelot

Lancelot, however, was a dangerous adversary whether armed or not. When Mordred and Agravaine banged on the door of the bedchamber, Lancelot, with his superior strategy, tricked one of the knights into entering. He quickly disarmed and killed him on the spot. Thus armed, he bade Guinevere lock herself inside the chamber and proceeded to fight all the twelve knights, whom he killed, including Agravaine. Though sorely wounded, Mordred escaped and rode to the King, informing him that he had found Lancelot in the Queen's bed and that it was a guilty Lancelot who had murdered the twelve unarmed knights and Agravaine.

Arthur was shocked to learn that Lancelot had acted in such a cowardly manner, but Mordred was a persuasive liar and Queen Guinevere was condemned to be burnt. Arthur could not bear to question her, and she was therefore condemned without being able to defend herself with the true account of events. Thus the handsome face of Lancelot, a true Champion of the Queen, reminded Arthur yet again of his earthly weakness – lack of wisdom.

Lancelot Rescues Guinevere

THE SERIES OF CAMEO SCENES HAS LEFT
Arthur feeling both elated and apprehensive as the dark crystal
begins to cloud over completely. Lancelot appears, riding
furiously across the landscape, having received news that
Guinevere had been condemned to be burnt at the stake. He
had hoped that Arthur would defend his Queen and dismiss
the false claim of adultery, but the death of thirteen of Arthur's
knights represented an attack on his authority as king.
Thirteen was also a symbolic number which represented the
division of the ritual year, the death of his knights being a
potent omen that the reign of the sun-king was nearing an end.

The uproar at court over the death of the knights had immediately set in motion a great division between the knights of the Round Table. Many supported Lancelot, and even Gawain, who had been grieved to learn about the death of his brother, Agravaine, refused to escort Guinevere to the stake.

The King then asked Gawain's two remaining brothers, Gaheris and Gareth, but they too at first declined to perform such a gruesome task. Gareth had loved Lancelot like a younger brother, but because of his loyalty to the King he decided to accompany Guinevere to the place of execution, along with his brother Gaheris, in the white habit of friars. They were thus unarmed, and treated her with kindness and respect. There were other knights, however, who had always envied and hated Lancelot, among them Sir Belliance and Sir Griflet. And so, with a large company of armed knights, Guinevere was taken to a remote hillside outside Camelot. The galloping figure of Lancelot remained in focus for what seemed like an eternity to Arthur, but as the spiral passage of time suddenly reversed perspective, so the galloping rider began to disappear into a distant speck on the horizon.

The Rescue

Arthur was not prepared for the scene of great fury and slaughter, with Guinevere at the stake surrounded by battling knights. Dressed in a simple shift, her lovely face streaked with tears, her figure cast a dramatic silhouette against a darkening sky. The earth itself appeared violently to erupt and quake at the sight. For in the Celtic ritual year, Guinevere represented the Celtic Earth Goddess, who controlled the seasons. Lancelot's anger at the sight of Guinevere so shamefully treated was awesome to behold. Though accompanied by but a few of his kinsmen, he charged upon the scene and slew a great many knights before they could raise their own swords. In this frenzy, he unwittingly killed Gaheris and Gareth, not recognizing them in their concealing robes. Lancelot's rescue of Guinevere exacted an awful price; apart from the death of many good knights of the Round Table, the kingdom was irretrievably divided.

When Lancelot learned afterwards that he had killed both Gaheris and Gareth, it pained him more than any grievous wound suffered in battle. Gawain, thereafter, swore a great oath of vengeance on Lancelot, and he rode with the King, who pursued Lancelot and Guinevere. They besieged the castle in the Land of the Joyous Gard, where Guinevere and

The Slaying of Gareth

Lancelot had retreated. Gawain demanded that Lancelot should meet him in single combat, but Lancelot, still grieving over the death of Gareth, met Gawain only lightly armed, which gave Gawain a greater advantage. But even so, Gawain could not defeat Lancelot. Matching sword strokes with Gawain, Lancelot held back from attacking him with any real force. This angered Gawain, who attempted to provoke Lancelot by calling him a cowardly knight, for his oath of vengeance demanded that one of them should die.

The last scene, depicting Guinevere at the stake, with all its bitter consequences, has always haunted Arthur and he begins to weep. The volcanic heart of the earth also starts to erupt, as the depths of Annwn emerge and draw back the veil which hides the dark deeds of mankind. The dark crystal falls from his hand into the fiery abyss, and Arthur knows that he must descend once again into the inner temple of the earth and reclaim his soul.

The Face of the Silent Watcher

The Silent Watcher's face appears above the disappearing horizon as Arthur kneels in prayer. His perilous descent into Annwn requires all his courage and faith, and this time he is determined to reclaim his queen and win her love. In ancient Celtic myth, it was Arthur's role as sun-king to descend periodically into the depths of Annwn in order to rescue trapped souls. In the ritual year, he was forever born again at the time of the winter solstice and he returned annually with a retinue of newly evolved souls who, like him, journeyed on the golden wheel – the Celtic symbol of reincarnation.

The battle between Lancelot and Gawain took place over many long months. Lancelot thought that by sorely wounding Gawain and then allowing him to recover from his wounds, he would eventually cause Gawain to withdraw. But in their last encounter Lancelot was forced to mortally wound Gawain, the King's nephew whom Arthur loved best among his knights, with the exception of Lancelot. The death of the King's sister's son in Celtic myth also symbolized the end of matriarchal supremacy or power.

Arthur Departs to the Underworld

WITH THE DARK CRYSTAL NO LONGER in his possession, Arthur stares blindly across the starry night sky for inspiration. A dazzling light from a distant star catches his attention as it appears to move towards him. The lovely face of the Goddess, Ceridwen, is suddenly unveiled, with her arms reaching out in the shape of golden wings which encompass the world. Arthur stands with his head bowed, as a quiet voice, a soft whisper, calls his name. 'Follow me, and I will safely guide you through your last great ordeal.' As Arthur looks up, a robed figure on horseback appears at the bow of his solar-ship, holding the reins of another horse, and beckons

Journey to the Underworld

him to mount. Although the figure is heavily veiled, Arthur glimpses the face of his sister Morgan, but as he is about to speak the veiled figure motions with her fingers across her lips to remain silent.

Arthur follows the veiled rider and they set off towards the bright star which has now moved ahead of them. After galloping across the expanse of night sky, their horses reach the horizon of the earthly realm, and Arthur feels a sense of relief and great expectation. The mysterious rider keeps a short distance in front, never turning once to see if Arthur, who has to ride hard to keep up, is following. They ride through the lands of Albion in the dead of night, all earthly life sleeping, and not a creature or sound stirs except for the lonely screech of the night-owl. Riding ever onwards, they come to a great wasteland, where the bright star suddenly stops and appears to rotate in a spiralling motion. The veiled figure reins up her horse and, from beneath her flowing cloak, produces a golden bow and arrow and presents them to Arthur.

The Golden Bow

In an instant the figure vanishes and Arthur finds that he is alone on a strange yet familiar hillside. He scans the horizon, trying to get his bearings, then realizes that he is inside a towering circle of stone giants. The sun is beginning to rise and it casts a thin beam of light between two of the huge stone pillars. Striking a smaller marker stone, a dramatic aura of sunlight lights up the circle. Arthur appears to be at the centre point of light, and the golden bow and arrow gleam with a radiance which mirrors the sun. Taking the arrow in his hand, Arthur draws back the bow and aims the arrow towards the rising sun, which is now directly overhead. The arrow soars upward and, in its flight, a shower of flames scatters far and wide over the earthly realm.

This age-old Celtic ritual symbolized the fertilizing role of sun-kings, who annually impregnated the Earth Goddess during the ritual year. Arthur had thus re-enacted his ancient role on earth, which meant that he could now journey to the Underworld to claim back Guinevere, his earthly bride and dual soul. The radiant light in the stone circle was beginning to dim, but two huge candles suddenly appeared in the sky and continued to cast a bright light over the world. The candles symbolized the Celtic fire festival of Brigantia, a time of the new moon which heralded new growth in the ritual year.

Arthur with the Three Queens

As Arthur's horse steps on the marker stone, a loud rumbling noise occurs and the stone begins to descend into the bowels of the earth, taking rider and horse with it. The air is thick with the smell of sulphur and a hazy mist engulfs him. Arthur shuts his eyes as he recalls another time when he travelled to the Otherworld, the place of light and life. He tries to retain this vision in order to remind himself that death is only the beginning of a new cycle of eternal life. The vision remains with him and three angels appear overhead, a heavenly presence that greatly strengthens his spirit.

One of the three queens carries a flaming torch, which again relates to Brigantia, the ancient Celtic ceremony which later transmuted into the Christian festival of Candlemas. Fire festivals, though lunar orientated, symbolized the changing seasons, which reflected the changing persona of the Earth Goddess. Guinevere represented the Celtic Earth Goddess who, like the Greek Persephone, had to endure a period of time in the Underworld. Arthur knew that his journey into this realm meant confronting his Dark Twin, who, in Arthurian myth, was represented by Mordred.

The Dark Twin

ARTHUR JOURNEYS THROUGH THE DARK passage leading to the Underworld and, as he opens his eyes, he becomes aware of a bright light ahead of him. In the far distance a ghostly White Castle rises from snow-capped mountains. The mystical scene draws him towards the great shining light, but it is too dazzling to gaze upon. He prays with eyes firmly shut, and asks God to bless his people and to give him the strength to overcome the dark evils of his kingdom. His spirit is suddenly freed from his earthly body and begins to rise above the White Castle. He finds himself on a high plateau with two lovely but unearthly maidens, each carrying a shining symbol of the Holy Grail – the chalice and the spear. A shaft of light pierces the ground between his feet to reveal his sword, Excalibur.

The White Castle

Grasping the sword, he thrusts it deep within the ground and immediately the vision of the maidens vanishes. He remains standing on the edge of a high precipice, a desolate place, as a howling wind screams wildly around him. Then silence. A strange echo of eerie laughter is followed by another deafening silence. A rasping voice, like that of the croaking raven, speaks: 'Dear brother, why doth thou still fear me?' Arthur remains frozen to the spot, but, summoning all his courage, he replies: 'Dear sister, step forward that I may see you.' The earth shakes violently and Arthur finds himself falling into the fiery abyss of Annwn.

The burning flames consume the remnants of his earthly shell, but his rising spirit floats to the top of a huge lake. Arthur looks up to the light of a crescent moon and begins swimming towards the shore. Suddenly he is held fast by invisible hands and sucked into a dark whirlpool. The distorted angry face of Mordred appears and Arthur has to exert all his remaining strength to free himself from Mordred's icy grip. Exhausted, he manages to reach the shore, where the Fate Goddess, Morgan le Fay, is waiting to greet him. She clasps his hands and pulls him effortlessly from the dark waters.

The Goddess of Fate

The duality of the soul, which manifests itself in a 'Higher Self' and a 'Lower Self', has long been mentioned in many ancient religions around the world. In Arthurian myth this duality was identified with Arthur and Guinevere, but the Dark Twin represents the soul's shadow-self, a totally separate entity. In earlier Celtic myths relating to sun-kings this shadow-soul was identified with a Dark God called Dis or Pwyll, the Dark Initiator, whose role was that of regenerating the spark of divinity within mankind.

In Arthurian mysticism Arthur's Dark Twin is represented by his son Mordred, for only by confronting the darker legacy of his bloodline, a residue within himself, can he win the Holy Grail – the symbol of eternal life. The timely intervention of the Fate Goddess symbolizes a reconciliation with the Mother Goddess, Ceridwen, who, according to Druidic belief, dwelt in the White Castle of Dinas Emrys, a secret city hidden within the Snowdonia mountain range. The abyss of Annwn was said to be situated in the depths of the castle's dungeons; its fiery breath came from golden dragons who also drew her chariot across the sky – an event linked to the blaze of comets which prophesied the birth of great sun-kings.

The Angel

Annwn was the primal place of fire whence all earth life had been formed. To return there was a reference to the druid's ancient belief in reincarnation, which allowed the soul to be born again. The symbol of the crescent moon relates to the Lunar Goddess, Brigantia, whose followers lit flaming torches to symbolize the fiery breath of the green dragon, an ancient symbol of new life.

The lakeside scene disappears and Arthur gazes upwards to the heavenly stars which sparkle all around him. A smiling angel looks down upon him and his spirit once again begins to soar among the stars. She signals him to follow her and, thus having defeated his Dark Twin, he begins his final journey across the vast galactic expanse towards the sun. *En route* he passes the planets, which had been but distant wandering lights on earth, as he winds his way like a speeding meteorite towards the golden circle of Gwynvyd, the place of 'Purity', identified in druidic cosmology with the sun. Here, he will be reunited with Guinevere.

Arthur Reunited with Guinevere

THE GALACTIC SPHERE IS A SPIRALLING circle of stars which form an intricate pattern in the night sky. Celtic knotwork reflects the complexity and integral 'oneness' of the universe with mankind. As Arthur stands before the entrance of Gwynvyd, the golden 'Circle of Creation', he has reached the divine point of immortality. The two figures kneeling at his feet symbolize the spiritual reunion of Arthur and Guinevere. It is a momentous point of mystical revelation for Arthur, who gazes ever onwards to the distant light of the White Swan constellation, home of the Celtic people's great creatrix. This 'Circle of Creation', known as Ceugant, was the

The Circle of Creation

galactic boundary in druidic cosmology which could never be crossed by mankind, for it symbolized 'Infinity' – a place beyond mankind's comprehension.

But a new era of space travel has begun, which may one day encourage space travellers to venture beyond our own solar system. In ancient Celtic myth, white swans symbolized the radiant divinity of the ancient gods. Today, psychologists are beginning to take mythology much more seriously in their study of the human mind, particularly with regard to ancestral memory or intuitive knowledge. Therefore, perhaps it is not too outrageous to suggest that the bright star Deneb in the White Swan constellation could be a relevant directional marker to other worlds. Arthurian myths create a powerful sense of mystery and intrigue which is not confined to the romance of the period. The figure of Merlin embodies an external force or an invisible entity, working secretly in the background as the 'Universal Alchemist'.

Arthur and Guinevere stand together at the entrance of the White Chapel; the doors have opened to reveal the Holy Grail. They step forward, holding hands, reunited as true lovers always are in the realm of the Celtic Otherworld. Arthur has reclaimed his bride and the deep chasm of time which had divided them over countless centuries has been crossed. Their reunion symbolizes the healing powers of the Holy Grail, a potent symbol of ancient spiritual belief which, like Arthur, had to struggle to survive. While spiritual concepts need to evolve, the source of faith flows from the sacred well deep within the soul. Ancestral memory is a powerful influence within us all and, as humanity struggles towards another millennium, this vision of Arthur and Guinevere perhaps symbolizes our hopes and dreams.

Merlin had compared the Round Table to the world – an apt analogy in view of human drama that continues to unfold around the world. Arthur's kingdom was destroyed by human passions and conspiracies, and the court of Camelot epitomizes the complex nature of social behaviour and the archetypal personalities it produces. Thomas Malory lived at a time when court intrigues and power struggles were linked in the Wars of the Roses (1455–85), a devastating English civil

Arthur and Guinevere at the White Chapel

war. He was a knight who changed his allegiance and fought on both sides. While imprisoned in the Tower of London, awaiting either his pardon or his execution, he wrote an inspirational account of the Arthurian saga. He had been charged with a number of crimes, including rape and sedition – a true Merlin figure.

The prophecies of Merlin, recorded in 1136 by Geoffrey of Monmouth in his extraordinary book *The History of the Kings of Britain*, make compelling reading with regard to the destiny of mankind. Apart from predicting the rise and fall of Hitler, predating a similar Nostradamus prophecy by several centuries, the prophecies mention a future Channel Tunnel link between England and France. Merlin also prophesied underwater exploration which would divulge the secrets of all the creatures that live under the sea. This particular feat will, apparently, cause great fear among mankind – but no explanation is given, except for a tentative link with an Atlantean civilization.

Arthur with Excalibur

Both Monmouth and Malory refer to ancient records with regard to their sources; this is generally thought to mean the 'oral tradition' of the British and Irish Celtic races, which was still very much part of everyday life during their historical periods, for only a few nobles and the clergy were literate in the sense of being able to read and write. The last prediction speaks of rising seas and the battling elements of nature as signs of ill-omen around the world. All ancient prophecies foretell increasing evils and another great deluge or natural disaster taking place at some time in the future.

But the conflict between good and evil, according to druidism and many Eastern religions, will continue until the end of time. For without the challenge of overcoming evil, humanity would quietly slip into a very different world – the Celtic Otherworld of the Sidhe, or the Faery kingdom. Wondrous place of light it may be, but it remains a place of dreams. The enigmatic figure of Arthur provides one last memory of the nobility of the human soul. With Excalibur safely back in his hands, the battle against the evils in the world may now recommence, with great victories in prospect.

The King

Further Reading

A selected bibliography of Arthurian and related titles

Davis, Courtney, *The Celtic Art Source Book*, Blandford, London, 1988 and 1989

—, *Celtic Borders and Decoration*, Blandford, London, 1992

—, *The Art of Celtia*, Blandford, London, 1993

de Troyes, Chrétien, *Arthurian Romances*, translated by W. Comfort, Everyman, New York, 1978

Eschenbach, Wolfram von, *Parzifal*, translated by H. M. Mustard and C. E. Passage, Knopf Inc., New York, 1961

Evans, Sebastian, *The High History of the Holy Grail*, Dent, London, 1910

Geoffrey of Monmouth, *The History of the Kings of Britain*, translated by Lewis Thorpe, Penguin Books, Harmondsworth, 1966

Jung, Emma and Marie Louise von Franz, *The Grail Legend*, Sigo, Boston, 1986

Knight, Gareth, *The Secret Tradition in Arthurian Legend*, Aquarian, Wellingborough, 1983

Lacey, Norris J. (ed.), *The Arthurian Encyclopaedia*, Garland, New York, 1986

Malory, Sir Thomas, *Le Morte D'Arthur*, Everyman, 1906

Matthews, John, *King Arthur and the Grail Quest*, Blandford, London, 1994

Matthews, John and Marian Caitlín, *The Grail Seeker's Companion*, Aquarian, Wellingborough, 1986

Matthews, John and Bob Stewart, *The Warriors of King Arthur*, Blandford, Poole, 1987

—, *Legendary Britain*, Blandford, London, 1988 and 1990

Skeels, D., *Romance of Perceval in Prose*, University of Washington, Seattle, 1966

Stewart, R. J., *The Book of Merlin*, Blandford, Poole, 1987 and 1988

—, *Merlin and Women*, Blandford, Poole, 1988

—, *Celtic Gods, Celtic Goddesses*, Blandford, London, 1990

—, *Celtic Myths, Celtic Legends*, Blandford, London 1994

Stewart, R. J. and J. Matthews, *Merlin Through the Ages*, Blandford, London, 1995

Tennyson, Alfred, Lord, *Idylls of the King*, Signet, 1961

Other Blandford titles
by Courtney Davis

The Celtic Art Source Book
Celtic Borders and Decoration
The Art of Celtia
Celtic Saints
Celtic Mandalas

For further information on the art of Courtney Davis write to:
3 Rodden Row, Abbotsbury,
Dorset DT3 4JL, enclosing four first-class stamps.

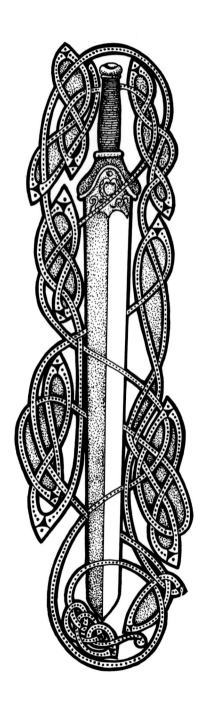